WORDS:
POWER, STRENGTH, INSPIRATION

EBŌNEE M. OLIVER

ISBN-13:978-0996025140
ISBN:0996025146

Printed in the United States of America
First Printing February 2018

Words: Power, Strength, Inspiration

CONTENTS

To my paternal grandfather, James Oliver, Sr.

Papa, I miss you so much. I will always strive to make you proud!

Acknowledgments

God, I am grateful for the gift you've given me, and I vow to be a good steward! Thank you for anointing me to write this book full of poetry. I am honored to be used by you!

My beautiful and amazing parents, Robert & Mareen Oliver, Sr.

Thank you for raising me "right." I am who I am today because of you two! Mommy, thank you for being my biggest fan. I'm positive my gift of writing came from you! We are both authors now!! Daddy, thank you for being my listening ear and confidant and for encouraging me to write. You both have helped my self-esteem tremendously. I am truly blessed to be Robert & Mareen's daughter. My love is never ending for you two. THANK YOU from the top of my heart! I hope always to make you proud.

My siblings, Robert Oliver, Jr. (R.J.) my little everything, I'm so glad I have you as a brother! Thank you for always encouraging me in whatever I do, I love you deeply.

Qiana Monique, True, thank you so much for always being present and assisting me in this journey! Your expertise in writing and spoken word execution is exceptional! Sister, you are a brilliant mind!! Thank you for inspiring me and pushing me forward! I love you immensely!

My grandparents, Daisy Peoples, Everett Oliver, and Lee & Katherine Peoples. You four have my heart. Thank you for loving me. I am a grateful granddaughter. I love you all.

My spiritual mother, Dr. Tiffany K. Jordan. Thank you for motivating me and being the first to encourage me to write a poetry book. Thank you for being my midwife and helping me effortlessly! You are one of a kind, and I'm so blessed and honored to have you in my life. Thank you for caring more about my purpose and destiny than my feelings. I appreciate every rebuke and impartation, this book is literally prophesy fulfilled! Thank you Mom! I love you.

The Anointed Harvesters, maisha r carter, my big sister, my mentor, my life coach, Thank you for believing in me, pushing me, developing me and encouraging me. Through my many transitions and accomplishments, you have been right there every step of the way. You love me like your own, yet guide me as your sister. I'm blessed to have you in my life. I love you, Mai :)

Shebeta Carter, I appreciate you loving me the way you do. You have helped guide me in ways you wouldn't even believe. Thank you for accepting me and allowing me to glean and learn from you. Your support means so much to me. I love you "MoMe."

Introduction

What you are about to indulge in, is some of the first poems I have ever written!

As this book was being written I had several revelations of how important our words are. Everything you speak out of your mouth has power. Your words are your strength! What are you speaking into the atmosphere? Who are you inspiring?

My hope and prayer is that each poetic writing and story blesses you and that you live your best life from this moment forward.

With Love,
Ebonee

Words

Actions speak louder than words, but words are more than just nouns and verbs that we use in a sentence, articulate in an instance, and can be heard from near or far away distance.

Your words have the ability to build someone up or tear someone down, so that means every word you speak should probably be profound.

Don't look down on those who choose to use words of life, and glorify those whose words lead to strife.

People have told you that "Sticks and stones may break your bones, but words will never hurt you." Well, that can't be true because death and life lie in the power of the tongue, and seeing that is the case, I see why so many die young.

They speak words that so slowly come to pass, not realizing that they have destroyed their own paths. They use words that make them laugh, that they think have no true meaning and mock others who use words wisely, like for interceding.

Those who downplay words and don't understand their true power will end up falling just like the tower with a weak foundation; words were used at the beginning of creation; God spoke into existing what He was creating.

You're making yourself believe every word you have spoken, whether it's for you to be healed or whether it's for you to remain broken.

There is a law to confession; this is more than a brief lesson. For those who don't agree, I don't mean to bring frustration.

But I believe if you grasp this we can change nations with our words. We can declare that things be not as though they were and even though things may occur, we have been given power to make a difference.

Please listen, I'm on a mission to shed wisdom and explain the impact of which your words can be.

To show, you can be free at last, from your current situations by speaking words of life into your destinations, and helping to transform this generation.

But first, you need to acknowledge that words were used in the beginning and words will be used now, until the very ending of time.

Do not be blind to what you know is true. Because what you speak out of your mouth is truly what you will produce.

Proverbs 18:21 *Death and life are in the power of the tongue*

Wake Up

There are many who are changing faces, in different places, and revealing hidden phases. Love or hate. Deal or procrastinate. Scared to say, "Jesus," heathens mock us because they think we're fake, they don't believe us.

We need to stand up and be a witness, repent and ask for forgiveness and be true Christians, not fans of religion. We need to make a decision and lead by example and recruit. Who we really are will surely be revealed through our fruit! There's no dispute, make a choice, your voice does have rule.

Rules weren't meant to be broken they were given as tokens to help you improve, not lose. Girls sleeping around with dudes misusing their tool. Dudes acting like fools to prove that they are ready to move and produce.

All failing in the school of life, cruising along to the same song of "I have time." Let me tell you; you don't have time. The clock is ticking, without your permission, please listen to wisdom, she's crying out.

She's been crying since the beginning, but you reject her. She comes in uniform and stands upright in the right form, this isn't foreign to you.

I'm reminding you that you have to choose life or death. Make a choice.

Too many fake prophets around prophesying but all they do is profit lies because they won't study the truth. They feed into what is produced by others to make it seem like they're hungry when really, they are content with being mediocre.

Wake up Church, the truth hurts. We need to be better; the weather is changing. Christians blowing in the wind, pretending to make it rain, twirling in the snow, dying slow, spreading gossip and pain, and telling their brothers to stay in their own lane.

I am my brother's keeper; I keep praying, I know the world is watching waiting and looking forward to us messing up. I'm giving you a charge, from the God in charge of heaven.

People say wake up, go forth with your dreams, and that's true. You need to wake up, dream and fulfill the vision God has planned for you; especially this year. The end is coming sooner than you think, just like in a rear-view mirror; things are closer than they appear.

1 Peter 4:7 NIV *The end of all things is near*

Still I Rise

Conviction so deep, ocean floors, wouldn't even compete with the depth of it. With sightings of gravestones saying, "Rest In Peace." Reflections in the mirror, I saw me, not you.

Seen as a child, content with milk because milk was safer to swallow, and no effort to chew. Meat wasn't hard to eat, that wasn't the real issue. I was so stuck on being mediocre, that authentic growth was something I wasn't used to.

On this quick path to hell, because heaven seemed too far, you don't realize how far you have fallen, until you see where you really are. Words written in red and black, but never read. Ignoring what was there, acting if I didn't care and nothing was ever said.

The thought of being dead wasn't a problem. Even though opting out of eternal damnation was the plan. Serving not God, but man.

Walking on shaky ground, feeling like sand, looking around town, and still found no steady land. Sinking each chance, I get to stand on my own two feet. Trying not to repeat the same cycle.

Feels like I've run my course, I won't file for divorce, so I continue on my journey. No need to hurry or worry. I got time right, time will tell, how long this tale will last.

Time is passing; it's not waiting for me. Knowing right from wrong, feeling empty, when simply all I have to do is repent.

Intensely, feeling weaker as time goes on. This conviction in my heart has shown me, that I was wrong and I need to be right. I stand humbly as a reflection of His light to say, "God, I apologize; you can have my life."

Ecclesiastes 7:8 NRSV *Better is the end of a thing than its beginning*

Fearless

I am unashamed of the gospel of Christ, for it is the power unto salvation to all those, who believe. I have faith as a grain of mustard seed. I can do all things through Christ who strengthens me. For God has not given me the spirit of fear, but of power, love and a sound mind.

The Lord is my light and my salvation, whom shall I fear, NO ONE! Perfect love drives out fear, and I am loved by the Creator! I am unstoppable; nothing is impossible to me.

Everything my hand touches prospers. I can do anything. I am the product of a King. I am fearfully and wonderfully made. My life was blood paid, on Calvary.

I traded fear, for faith. I am confident; I am bold as a lion. I am great because the greater one lives within me. My father loves me; I am the object of his affection.

My obedience is my protection; His love kills rejection. I am wise; I've eliminated deception, I've changed since conception, since I've made a powerful confession.

Scripture says, "Touch not my anointed, and do my prophets no harm." I am not worried because I am armed, with the breastplate of righteousness, the shield of faith, which quenches all the fiery darts of the wicked. I will never quit. I am assigned to this; my eyes are open.

I represent the highest God. This is not a job; this is my purpose, my kingdom assignment. I am priceless, far from worthless. I know who I am. I am the righteousness of God. I stand firm in my vow. I am fearless.

2 Timothy 1:7 NKJV *For God has not given us the spirit of fear*

Release

Every time my mouth is open and a word is spoken, God has chosen to move within me, because I invited Him to live on the inside of me; a King, who reigns supreme over everything, who created and dated His workmanship, Who puts gifts on display for His glory.

Hands are lifted and raised; mouths open filled with praise. Let me tell you if you had 10,000 tongues it still wouldn't be enough to say, "Thank you, Lord."

The one who made you from pure dirt and put you on this earth for such a time as this, don't dismiss an opportunity to worship Him, learning Him is the greatest amount of time you can spend.

Everyone else knows your sins and pretends to forgive you. But the living truth says, "Repent and turn away; everything will be ok, trust me. Let me lead you and guide you, rest in me, believe in me. I am He who heals, and fulfills every promise."

The most honest, the one who gave sight to the blind, who turned water into wine, who's always on time, who died and rose, and proposed to His own body, and married them happily so you could be free.

The alpha and omega, the beginning and the end, the realist friend, the one who is more attractive than all men who say that they are God.

His patience and holiness shows how much He loves us. How He always thinks of us, He can deliver you from anything, lust, pride, and rebellion.

What I'm saying is God is amazing, the best encounter you can have on this planet is him. Better than, the best diamond, or priceless gem. Our hearts are what

He wants to take and mend. Truly the ending is when we are finished and we allow him to begin.

Psalm 150:6 NKJV *Let everything that has breath praise the Lord*

Journey

Open wider than the Pacific Ocean; details detected. A specific vision never closed, doors knocked upon, and houses responded.

It is said that no one knows or even comes close to understanding someone, who is willing to host such a powerful event. Words taken meant for reasonable value, interesting how you walk by, crying, reminiscing on love.

Doves flew by effortlessly to show the newness of us. Trust connected, and prevented error, despite the terror of false conviction; my heart listened when you spoke.

I choked on gossip because it wasn't meant for me to digest. Impressed on your nature at first, situations later gave me a heads up on you. Only a person of high value could gasp me. Relating to former views in conversations had me confused. What's the use if I'm going to be used, I don't enjoy being abused.

I don't want to lose this round of life; I've sacrificed half my life to get to this point. I don't want to be disappointed even though you're not permanent. Expectations have failed, rejection has tried to come in, but I blocked it with my bat of wisdom. Realizing in kitchens things get stirred up and boiled over. Lesson learned; slow down from this day forward.

Proverbs 14:12 NKJV *There is a way that seems right to a man*

Our Love

Our love was founded on purity and spiritual maturity. God's hand placed on a set of people willing to be used by Him. The example of holiness and sanctification gave revelation on why this covenant was created.

Mandated by the souls crying out for wisdom, two beautiful hearts willing to listen to God's provision. It visited, left marks, and gave free will charts for the hearts that He knew would agree. The blood He shed on Calvary, gave us love endlessly, that our covenant would be heaven made, blood paid, and earthly laid for us to enjoy.

So beautiful, God's hand placed on an unbreakable unit, the sight of honesty renewed in the earth. The greatest love of all, besides His death and resurrection, was us. He trusts that we will honor and obey His command, this three-ring strand is not easily broken because the third person is God and not man.

You may not fully understand the power of marriage, however, it's more than sex and carats and honeymoons in Paris. It's about the true value of two people coming together for God's purpose and learning how He desires for them to dominate in His kingdom.

Watch and see where God will take you when you have His blessing; don't guess it, just receive because we're excited, and we believe it.

Mark 10:8 NKJV *and the two shall become one flesh*

Process

We want our eyes to be opened, but we will choose to stay blind to truth. Too many times we have been introduced to lies in our lives, and we spend time trying to categorize what's right, what's wrong, what's too deep and what's not deep enough. We are distracted, my people.

The earth itself is an evil place to some of us. However, I've never seen so many Christians angry at one another. People calling folks false prophets without having a real definition of what a prophet is. Everybody wants a title, and feels entitled to a platform, who are you?

Last time I checked, a check didn't make you. God did. Wealth and riches don't justify holiness. Holiness needs no justification; it just is. Take heed to revelation. What are you doing with your life? Who are you trying to please? Are you attempting to appease yourself? STOP! God needs you!

He needs your heart to be right, your mouth to be right, even your body. Not just healthy. But pure. I'm not perfect whatsoever; however, I know you've been hiding. I've hid before too.

I'm saying this because I love you. Stop touching death and expecting life. Stop eating poison and expecting nutrition. Time is of the essence; we don't have time to waste.

What will it take—killings, bombs—for us to wake up. Everything we've tried to escape from we've become. No one is exempt; honestly, I promise it will help if we get back to what's important. Jesus.

He is the answer to everything in every situation. Don't hesitate to put Him back at the forefront. Don't front. You need Him. You don't have all the answers. Because you didn't create you.

Let's all come together for the good, let's not get weary in well doing. Let's be all we can be. Beautiful and creative. Humbly.

Matthew 6:22 *The light of the body is the eye: if therefore thine eye be single, thy whole body shall be full of light*

My Ex

It was as if I were in a familiar realm, I gave him my heart. He was my Romeo, and I was his Juliet, only he didn't have to audition for the part. I just let him in as my friend; he put my heart in his hands, and he was immature so, he drew on it and called it romance.

I finally have the chance to tell this man, that I'm worth more than someone who creeps and does nasty dances in the street and french kisses with his friends in the park. I'm more than his female mistress he wants to tempt after dark. I am nothing that he has ever seen; I'm a queen! I was born to conquer! I am better than this!

I refuse to let this drive me to hell. I know it sounds suspicious well, there's a story I have to tell. The journey began to unfold, and boldly he approached me, I liked physical touch, so I let him get close to me.

Who knew that this was the key to unlocking me. Freedom was freely given, consequently rejecting what is holy because I refuse to be lonely. Science connected our chemistry; history is how we have seen each other, math added another class to give philosophy on us.

This relationship is deeper than what the average eye can see. It's circled around this person, someone who tried to take advantage of me—someone I used to love and trust. Let me expose who he is; he is my ex. I called him "L," but you would call him Lust.

Time and time again he has tried to overtake and rape all the wisdom I knew about him. After years of our intimate gatherings between screens and human beings, I realized his job was to devour me. I was flowered with his confidence, which gave me none at all.

Surrounded by towers of false humility, pride always took the wheel. First quarters don't always dictate the fourth. I wasn't taken by surprise though; I was mesmerized. Somebody wanted me. He wanted me. Seduced by a lie itself I ended it, by saying no thank you. I'm leaving you for good; I'm finished. I'm choosing to allow and represent somebody else. Goodbye.

Galatians 5:16 NIV *So I say, walk by the Spirit, and you will not gratify the desires of

the flesh*

Naked

I am perceived to believe how I am seen as a human being, even though; it is not what I see. I am me, yes, beautifully made, handcrafted by the very best. Yet, seeds of incest crept in, and my emotions were a wide door that let lust walk in. Who knew, such damageable tasks that I was partaking in ,would give me consequences that would change the way I viewed myself within.

I couldn't pretend like I liked one sex, at the time it was more like one and a half. People judge honesty, but honestly, I don't care; this started as a child being curious. People say curiosity will kill you; they're right. It tried to kill me softly, and instead of killing my flesh, I accepted what was handed to me as if it was God's best.

The first kiss dismissed every ounce of conviction I had in my heart; being felt upon, no more private parts. The second kiss was an entrance, where I felt like my interest was trying to be changed. So many nights, I remember summer months, June, July and August into September, thinking about his words and her actions. Being young and dumb, being told it's not all my fault.

I agreed, even though we were caught portraying what television views as entertainment. Who knew what I was viewing was tainted; it was as if I had made arrangements to accept the payments for my enslavement.

He was the first encountered, and she was the second. She was more than just a thought, more like an open idea. I wanted to touch what had never been touched to see if that touch is what I wanted it to be; that experience wasn't for me. Secretly, thinking no one would know what was happening sexually.

Growing older frustrated, mandated to be an example, thinking, "Why now, I have ample time." I was so blind as I stood in line, front row of the choir.

With hiding my sin, a few inquired, but I lied, saying my struggle expired.

In my heart, I desired to be free but didn't feel like freedom could ever live within me. Dreaming of the day when the bell would ring, where I could graduate and go on to the next thing. It was so interesting, I felt like no one would catch me. Caught too many times in the middle, I loved the touch of wicked, as if it tickled my body a little.

I enjoyed the place of bondage, but knew I couldn't stay there. I was wearing blindfolds like they were prescription glasses. Realizing that I couldn't see, even though the light is on and near me. I am disturbed by secrets the evidence is leaking, looking around there's only one treatment, fleeing from this.

Expose what's been proposed, undress what's been clothed, accept what has gotten old. Telling the truth about the real me, that no one knows. Some of my struggles, not being able to choose between dressing like a man or woman, being controlled by an object and a screen, remaining damned or being redeemed.

Let me tell you, don't allow yourself to be trapped to a secret. Reveal what's never been said—someone needs it; healing will follow. Don't wait until tomorrow; it's not promised. Don't hide behind the tree, be free, be empty. Freedom is yours, accept it and receive it. For you have been made with great purpose, your story continues. Keep moving forward victory is yours, you will succeed, because who God makes beautifully, He beautifully redeems.

John 8:36 AMP *So if the Son makes you free, then you are unquestionably free*

Free

I just wanna be different. I don't want to live in prison by trying to be somebody else. I'd rather be by myself than to die a copy. I'm original; this content is for the ear that will listen, that's missing something, their own life, whose sacrificed so much, just to stay in touch with society.

Well, the reality is they didn't create you. They will love you, hate you, and disown you. They want to clone you for personal gain, causing you to embrace pain, and participate in the game of manipulation.

But let me tell you. You don't have to play because someone was willing to pay for you. The one who is the living truth, the one that produces one-of-a- kind creations. Satisfaction guaranteed. The one that gives identity, the one—a part of the Trinity. Jesus. The most original being to ever step foot on this earth.

Born from a virgin, something never heard of. The greatest love ever mentioned is when Jesus died and rose, not only so that you can have Eternal Life, but so you can appreciate, the life He gave you.

He made you unique, don't insult His creativity by trying to be the generic version of who He made. Everything that you were born with was meant to be, but if there is anything related to a curse, reverse it and send it back to the enemy.

He can't create, he only can copy. You wonder why you can't fit in. Let me tell you; you're neatly made, putting on a facade is pretty sloppy. But I encourage you to be free in your originality, but be bold as a lion, because when you walk like you're supposed to, it will be easy, without you even trying. In the end, I hope your eyes are open so you can see. That from now until eternity I'm free to be me.

Psalm 139:14 *** I am fearfully and wonderfully made***

Obedience

Obedience ain't popular, but it's right. How many times have you ran like Jonah hoping to get swallowed by a whale, so that you wouldn't have to go through with it? Let's be honest. It's hard to say no when you don't know what's on the other side.

Lack of trust and false expectations will cause you to overthink every time. Like math problems, you want to add two plus three to get five, and God wants fourteen minus nine to get you in line. To show you His way is best, yes, we can agree we're intelligent.

He created us. We were created by the Creator, whose most creative at creating creatives despite what you believe, yet and still He knows what's best. Like Adam, distracted by your rib. Let me tell you! Whatever God has told you to do, do it. If He told you to get moving, move it. If He told you to pursue, pursue it. If He told you to fast, fast and if He tells you to laugh then laugh.

Freedom. I've never felt this free in my life. I'm coming to you as a poetic midwife to tell you that your obedience will keep you. Disobedient children don't live long, and because we're made spirit first, I don't want you to die wrong.

Wide is the pathway to destruction and narrow is the path to eternal paradise. Your life is not a game, not like rolling dice—much more precise. If you can't trust the one who holds your future, then what is life?

Give up your right to be right. You're wrong. It doesn't have to be short when it's meant to be long. Take heed to the poem, listen to the song. The heartbeat of heaven is calling. Will you answer the phone?

John 14:15 NRSV *If you love me, you will keep my commandments*

The key to my success in life has been my close relationship with Jesus Christ. He is the reason for my existence and purpose. I encourage you to search your heart today, ask yourself, "If I left this earth today, where would I spend eternity? What will the end of my story look like? What would life with Jesus look like?"

Having a personal relationship with Christ gives such a sense of security and assurance. I am confident that just like He changed my life, He can change yours.

He is waiting with open arms to be your Savior, and to be your God.

Prayer of Salvation

I come to you just as I am. You are the only true and living God. I ask you to forgive me, I repent of my sins. I believe Jesus Christ is the son of God, who out of obedience to the Father, died for my sins and was raised from the grave. I ask you to enter my life, live in me and through me from this day forward. I acknowledge you as Lord of my life from this moment forward; I belong to you. Thank you for loving and accepting me. In Jesus name, amen.

Biography

Ebōnee M. Oliver is a fresh voice emerging from a new generation of leaders. Having spent most of her adolescence honing her skills in the Church and the local community, the Chicago native has a passion for both ministry and the performing arts. First, a lyricist creating her own rhymes, Ebōnee easily transitioned to writing poetry as an outlet in 2011, and now flows comfortably between performing as an actor, spoken word artist and in stage/film production. Her reputation for being a proficient, resourceful, dependable and hardworking production assistant has allowed her the opportunity to work beside some Hollywood and gospel greats. She has had the honor of working with the highly acclaimed actor/director/producer Robert Townsend, GRAMMY and Stellar Award-winning recording artist Donald Lawrence and world-renowned Walt Whitman & The Soul Children of Chicago. As a lyricist and spoken word artist, she has performed in numerous New Year's Eve productions, video promos, music release parties, college events, as well as collaborated with Dwayne Wade's Wade World Foundation.

After a long-standing internship with The Anointed Harvesters, a theater and arts nonprofit, Ebōnee started her own production company in 2014, Let Your Light Shine Productions, which name reflects her life's motto based on the scripture Matthew 5:16. Let Your Light Shine Productions specializes in stage, event and social media management for both individuals and organizations.

Ebōnee also enjoys mentoring youth and is the former president of the Student Ambassador Program under Teen-Train, Inc., a Chicago-based nonprofit organization.

Ebonee is a new author who has released her first book of poems entitled "Words: Power, Strength, Inspiration" which is available now online.

She is excited about inspiring lives through her art and looks forward to helping to change the world one WORD at a time.

Connect with Ebōnee

Facebook & Periscope: Ebōnee M. Oliver

Instagram & Twitter: @eboneemoliver

For all speaking engagements and bookings, please send all inquiries to:
eboneeoliverbooking@gmail.com

In Loving Memory, of my cousin, Shaunklin Williams, my uncle, Stevenson Jones, my friend Meghan Steward and Pastor Forrest Dukes Sr.

www.ingramcontent.com/pod-product-compliance
Lightning Source LLC
Chambersburg PA
CBHW072057040426
42447CB00012BB/3155